Tong-len
The Alchemy of Reaction

by

Michael Erlewine

ISBN-13:
978-1516951147

ISBN-10:
151695114X

© Copyright Michael Erlewine, 2012-2015

CONTENTS

A Movable Feast 3
The Alchemy of Reactions 7
Reaction Toning 14
Response-Ability 18
Reactive Alchemy 21
Sending and Receiving: Tong-len 27
Tong-len: How I came to Learn It 33
Tong-len: Mental Feng-Shui 38
What about Hate and Fear? 41
Overload 44

A Movable Feast

This article is on what is called Relative Bodhicitta, the heart of the lion, so to speak, and it is where most of us are or will be for quite some time with our mind training. Relative Bodhicitta is all about working with our ego or Self in an attempt to diminish its strength.

This is not an easy task because the Self is exactly as clever as we are. After all, the Self is our own creation, the step-child of our attachments, a kind of zombie made up of our likes and dislikes.

The Self hangs on to what it has, to whatever it has drawn around itself, its coat of many attachments. Above all, it does not like to have anything taken away from it because it is used to always growing ever larger, not smaller.

The Self keeps what it likes and loves close, and what it does not like or hate at a distance. In that sense the Self is a living example of conservatism, doting on the status quo and resisting all change from the outside. The Self, like former president George W. Bush, thinks of itself as "The Decider," and likes to be in complete control.

At the same time, as clever as it may be, it is as dumb as a stone. About the only approach that works with the Self are some forms of reverse-psychology. So there you have a brief sketch of the Self. Sound familiar?

"The Seven Points of Mind Training," what is called Lojong, is a very deliberate method designed to deconstruct the Self and lessen its influence on us. This method takes time, but it actually works.

Regardless of whatever other Buddhist practices we do, every dharma path, like the Grand Central Station, seems to first pass through Lojong, "The Seven Points of Mind Training," at least in our lineage of Tibetan Buddhism, the Karma Kagyu. And the key to all of this deconstruction of the Self is the practice of Tong-len, which is also called "Taking and Sending" and "Exchanging Yourself for Others." We could call it "Self-Exchange," because, like the old game of Pick-Up-Sticks, with Tong-len we remove one bit of self-attachment after another and exchange it for what we thought of as 'other'.

And we don't have to feel sorry for our self because we are weakening it because the Self has no permanent existence. It not an entity, but nothing more than the current collage or collection of our own interests, our likes, dislikes, hopes, and fears. As the description of this technique states, Tong-len is simply a way of exchanging our Self for others and "Other" in general using reverse-psychology.

Actually, it is more like enlarging our Self by converting what we now label as "other" into our Self, making friends with that "other," and finally including it as part of our Self, one item or other at a time. Scholars tells us that through this process we are removing duality and becoming non-dual in our outlook. Or they say that we are discovering the 'interdependency' of all things. I like to think that by doing Tong-len practice we are adding what was once labeled as "other" onto our Self (making friends with that other) until the Self finally gets so large that it implodes for lack of any comparison, i.e. lack of any more other. It just bursts like an overblown balloon. Either way, it is deemphasized and gradually becomes less and less of an obscuration of our mind.

I like to say that the Self becomes increasingly transparent until we can see right through it to the true nature of the mind itself. However we spell it, the Self, which always will be part of us since it is (at the very least) our scheduler (and hopefully not our best friend or advisor) is eventually seen as the shadow of us that it actually is, rather than our boss. But I digress.

Tong-len, as mentioned, is the systematic deconstruction of our Self, hopefully rendering it more transparent, at least enough for us to realize the true nature of the mind behind or obscured by it. The Self, once understood, need not be an obstacle. The goal of all mind training is to get us to the point where we can have a glimpse of recognition as to the true nature of the mind itself. As mentioned, Lojong is mostly concerned with what is called "relative truth," the relation of our imagined subject (Self and everything that is not a subject, not our Self, i.e. 'other' than us.

Tong-len is a form of a psychological differential-calculus that is concerned with the ever-changing perimeter or border between our Self and all that is outside of it or considered other than our Self. Through Tong-len training, gradually the constant reification of the Self grows weaker and weaker, and a sense of transparency allows us to begin to see through our own Self to the actual nature of our mind, which is behind it.

This is a gradual, but sure, process and a necessary step or preliminary to achieve what is called "Recognition" in Tibetan Buddhism, an important gateway to the actual path to Enlightenment. "Recognition" refers to the recognition of the true nature of the mind, something that has to be pointed out to us by a guru or teacher who has realization enough to do this.

However, before this is possible, the thick layers of obscurations accumulated by the Self's attachments, have to be gradually thinned out and removed. Although this can be done through many practices, there is general agreement that Tong-len and the Lojong practice, "The Seven Points of Mind Training" are the most effective way to do this.

The Alchemy of Reactions

The technique presented here I came up with after being prompted by the dharma teacher Daniel P. Brown, a psychologist (and Buddhist scholar) on the faculty of the Harvard Medical School, who suggested that in the Four Noble Truths, the word "suffering" might better be translated as "reactivity," thus the First Noble Truth, which is "The Truth of Suffering" might better be translated as the "The Truth of Reactivity. After that I spent some years practicing with my own reactions. I ran this technique past Khenpo Karthar Rinpoche, my teacher, for his comments and he said that it was a sound idea. I was glad to hear it, so I will be a little more forward about sharing it. Some have expressed wanting to know how this technique works, so here it is for those who are interested.

Tong-len was the first Tibetan Buddhist mind-training practice that I instinctively understood and warmed to. It was easy to do and I could do it anytime and anywhere; it was portable.

Somehow Tong-len seems intuitively American. We just get it. Perhaps everyone does. If there is a vaccine that is the antidote for an inflated ego, this is it. And like the perfect diet, you can eat all you want and still loose the weight of your attachments.

Instead of denying the self as so many techniques tend to do, Tong-len's genius is just the opposite. It gradually identifies more and more territory as your friend (part of yourself) until the Self implodes by inclusion instead of denial. It's like blowing up a balloon until it bursts of its own accord.

In other words, tong-len uses the self's natural tendency to become attached to defeat itself. It is a miracle cure for the egocentric.

Here is an introduction to what in my opinion is the easiest to learn meditation method, called "Reaction Tong-len" or "Reaction Toning."

The Kinds of Meditation

The kind of mediation practiced by Zen and Tibetan Buddhists is what is called "awareness" meditation, learning to allow the mind to come to rest in awareness -- becoming more aware. But here in America, we basically have the one word "meditation" to cover hundreds of existing mind-training techniques, and most of them are not awareness-oriented.

Meditation methods can be divided into what we might call uppers and downers. Downers relax us and uppers make us more aware. The Buddha's teachings actually combine the two such that we learn to relax or rest in awareness. Buddhist methods are all about awareness, being mindful and becoming more aware -- waking up.

As examples of other kinds of meditation, there are "absorption" meditations, where we go inside or are guided in one way or another – eyes closed. Awareness meditation is typically done with eyes open. And there are literally hundreds of meditation types that are basically relaxation therapies of one form or another.

In fact, meditation for many people simply means learning to relax. There is a somewhat subtle difference between this and the methods Buddha taught, which was to learn to relax "as it is," so to speak. However, the Buddha taught to allow the mind to relax and rest in awareness, not in relaxation itself. In other words, rest "as it is" means to rest in the awareness that always is, as in the awareness it takes to read this. Rest in this awareness that it takes right now to read this sentence, rather than the content (what it means) of this sentence. Think about that. If you don't know how or if you are currently meditating but not getting the results you hoped for, you can easily learn this technique. That is the idea.

Meditation Hurdles

One of the potential problems with learning meditation is that it takes time and practice. Few people have enough time and fewer yet like to practice. A chief hurdle for many folks is finding enough time in a day to practice. Meditation, like any technique, has to be practiced until it becomes almost second nature. For most this involves setting aside some time each day (or every day or so) to practice and learn meditation, which is not the same as actually meditating.

For those of us with busy schedules, often the first thing to get scratched from our daily "to do" list is our meditation practice. Practice of any kind takes effort and spiritual practice has the additional problem that we really have no idea (yet) of what the results or outcome of the training is or will be. We are doing this on spec, and this can be discouraging.

These and other obstacles often lead to would-be meditation practitioners giving up and abandoning their efforts to learn to meditate. This is a generalization, but occasional practicing of meditation every day or so for a short time is a difficult way to reach the critical mass necessary for meditation to a become spontaneous habit.

I am not suggesting practicing for a long time each day unless that is joyful to you. Instead, the great mahasiddhas suggest that we practice many short times. What is even more needed is some way to apply the meditation technique, not just for one-half hour every a day or so, but all the time in whatever we have to do. IMO, that is the ticket.

Practice Places

Typically, learning meditation technique, what is called "practicing," takes place in a quiet place, often a little cushion off in a corner of a secluded room, and so on. That is where the technique is learned until we are fluent and we can stop "practicing" meditation and instead actually begin to just meditate. It is like those little training wheels we had on our bike as a kid.

Practicing in a special room, on a cushion, when we can get to it for some bit of time each day (or every day or so) is like going to church on Sunday for an hour and expecting to get into heaven. Of course, every little bit helps, but given all the variables that can intervene, the amount of practice that accumulates may not amount to enough to reach the critical mass needed to become passionate about meditating.

Daily practice is fine, but too often there are several variables that can intervene and short-circuit our efforts.

These include not keeping to our schedule. Often what happens on a busy day is that the first thing that gets cut from my schedule is my meditation practice. Runner-up is that we just don't feel like it that day and are sure that "tomorrow" will be a better time to practice, or we don't feel like we know what we are doing or we are not getting any results, etc. The list goes on. In other words, other methods are needed.

Enter "Reaction Toning," a simple technique that can be done all day long during whatever our normal schedule requires and one that accumulates serious amounts of dharma practice at no extra expense in time or concentration. And, it is easy to do.

Karma

The whole idea of "karma" very much relates to meditation practice and I will explain why, and karma is simple to understand. Our every action has a result. This is simple physics. And we have all heard about "good" and "bad" karma, at least from our point of view. The good karma produces results that we like, while the bad karma makes life more difficult for us.

And there is a popular misconception about karma to the effect that karma mainly relates to the kinds of "sins" listed out in the Ten Commandments, like "Do not kill," "Do not steal," and so on. Of course that is "bad" karma, but there is a much greater source of difficult karma, in particular since most of us are not killing and stealing anyway. I call it micro-karma.

Micro-Karma

As mentioned, it is not just the big karma-forming actions (killing, stealing, etc.) that we should watch out for, but rather the myriad of small actions that we habitually do that create the bulk of our "bad" karma and which most folks have no idea they are accumulating. As mentioned, I call this our micro- karma.

The Tibetan Buddhists differentiate between skillful actions (which they call Skillful-Means) and un-skillful actions, those whose result impair or obscure our minds. When we think of skillful means, we think of intentional actions, but the vast bulk of the 'bad" karma we accumulate is "unintentional" only in that we are not aware of it, but it too has intent. Ignorance of natural law is no excuse for bad intentions.

Chief among our "unintentional" karma are the reactions we have to almost everything all day long. And by "reactions" I mean our knee-jerk reactions, those we apparently cannot control, mostly because we are not even consciously aware of them. Keep in mind that the name "Buddha" means awakened, the one who is aware. Buddhism is the method (and its practice) of becoming more aware, of waking up.

We react all day long, but are not aware that we are doing so. When we become aware of our reactions, we can learn to respond appropriately to them instead of just reacting involuntarily. Thus I am distinguishing here between our uncontrollable "reactions" and appropriate responses. And by "reactions" I am not talking about the kind of reaction we have when we place our hand on a hot stove.

Instead, I am speaking here of the myriad of reactions we have based on our personal likes and dislikes, our prejudice, bias, antipathy, aversion, repugnance,, enmity, etc. that we have built up over the years, mostly thanks to our Self.

The Self

I am not going to go deeply into the concept of the Self. I have a whole book on it for those who are interested. Instead, here I just want to sketch out how our self can affect the accumulation of karma by its many attachments, particularly what it does not like. In brief, the Self is a montage of our likes and dislikes that we draw around us like a coat of many colors, only here it is a persona of many attachments, positive and negative.

The Self does its best to pull everything it likes closer and to keep away (at arm's length) everything it does not like or does not identify with. We all know this. Anyway, the Self reacts to all that it does not like and those reactions are recorded like any other event in our mindstream. The problem is that these reactions are so constant and often so intense that they amount to an almost constant accumulation of karma all day long and even in our dreams at night. And the amazing thing is that we are not even aware that this is taking place, so successfully do we ignore it.

The controversial poet and New-Age harbinger Aleister Crowley penned the phrase "To snatch at a gnat, and swallow a camel." This is effectively what we do with the torrent of reactions we record as karma each day. We are unaware of it all and yet it probably is the single greatest cause of "bad" karma that we have.

As they say, "Karma burns twice," first when it occurs and adds to our obscurations and second when somewhere down the line its imprint has to be removed, expunged.

Luckily there is an easy way for us to address this problem and greatly reduce the amount of micro-karma we record and this is "Reaction Toning," also called "Reaction Tong- Len."

Reaction Toning

Reaction Toning is a complete dharma practice, one that can be done (and is best done) off-the-cushion. Best of all, it does not interfere or add extra time to our busy schedule and day. Personally, I do this all day long. And it amounts to a lot of practice getting done, something very few people achieve since they do not have the time. It's Dharma-on- the-Go, so to speak.

And Reaction Toning is easy to learn, something we can do "on the hoof" so to speak. All that is needed is to begin to be aware of our reactions, and there is no lack of opportunity since we react, literally, all day long. What reactions are we referring to? Literally all of them. For example:

The not-so-fiendly office worker that suddenly comes round the corner and confronts us, face-to-face. We may try to control our reaction, but just note it. Note the wince and the avoidance we can feel. What is that?

"That" is nothing more than our reaction, regardless of the cause. The cause may be our instinctual dislike for someone who has offended us. But whether they did something to us on purpose or not is not important. We can't control the outer world, but we can recognize our reaction to it and begin to tone that down. As one of my favorite songwriters Seth Bernard penned, "Make friends with the weather." This does not mean we are unmoved by it, but it is very possible to transform knee-jerk reactions into appropriate responses that do not record karma.

To do this requires that we first note the reaction when it occurs and then recognize the reaction as purely our own. Someone else may be causing it, but how we react is totally up to us. So, after recognizing we have reacted, we then own it as ours and acknowledge to ourselves that we alone are reacting. This is our reaction. We own it and because of that we can change and modify it. Once we have owned the reaction, that by itself may be enough for it to begin toning down. Eventually we learn to spot it every time it arises until it no longer arises. Instead we begin to respond to whatever input we receive in an appropriate way. Or we may even do a little traditional Tong-len with it, taking in the worst from outside (from that other person) and sending back out the best in us we can offer.

I find that merely recognizing and owning my reactions is usually enough right there to begin toning them down and de-emphasizing a particular reaction. The more often we do it, the less emphatic (or traumatic) it becomes. We make friends with it.

Imprint or Groove

Our every negative reaction, let's say to a person we don't like, deepens the groove or trace in our mindstream connected to them. In other words, repeatedly reacting to someone (or something) negatively etches an ever deeper groove in the mind that not only further obscures our mind, but also that someday will have to be removed if we want a clear mind. Think how long and how often these reactions occur. It is scary.

Multiply this by the thousands of reactions we have each day and you get the picture, a torrent of micro-karma that steadily accumulates to our disadvantage. And this micro- karma is not reserved just for people we react negatively to. Our reactions descend to even finer reactions. For example, we don't like that person's nose, scar, scarf, color, or hat. Those too are faithfully recorded in our mindstream. "No reaction is too small" might be the motto here.

In other words, our daily reactions amount to thousands of tiny razor cuts, moments when we automatically wince, that record themselves as karma in our mindstream.

And the amazing thing is that with just a little work we can tone down and eventually remove those reactions and stop recording so much karma. And the byproduct of that is that our mind gradually clears up and we become increasingly more aware. In other words, this is a method to remove the effects of our "bad" karma and to stop recording it. And that is something to consider.

Another plus is that this technique is not rocket science. Anyone can do it and getting started is as easy as your next negative reaction, which probably will be coming along any second. And unlike many forms of meditation training, we can see and experience our progress with Reaction Tong-len right away, on the spot. It is a get-paid-as-you-go practice. As we come to terms with each reaction, we can allow the mind to just rest in the space or gap that appears as we own our reactions and they lessen in strength. We embrace them as oppotunities.

And since the process is pretty much instantaneous, we are not losing any time. In fact, we gain time because we are not embroiled in all the wincing, bobbing & weaving, and dodging that we usually do when we react negatively to something. We accumulate time and awareness as we go along.

As to how this method differs from its big brother Tong-Len, Reaction Tong-len is all about the Self and does not involve others as so many dharma practices do. The Buddhists are very clear that until we enlighten ourselves, we cannot enlighten others. Reaction Toning is like that old kid's game of Pick-Up-Sticks, gradually removing our own obscurations, one-by-one. And what is being removed through Reaction Toning is just that which separates us from others, all of the harsh criticism, bias, prejudice, etc., which is mostly directed at other people. So, Reaction Toning is about removing the "other" in our own self, which translates to an ever more inclusive embrace of everything "else" -- the end of dualism.

Response-Ability

I am taking off my story-telling hat and putting on my didactic hat because I keep running across folks in my life that have managed to paint themselves into one corner or another because they react instead of respond. It makes me want to comment, and I am.

I have been counseling for something like 45 years now and I want to share with you what I find to be a key factor in that experience. Much of what takes place in a counseling session boils down to how a person responds to what is happening to them in their life. We can't control what others say and do to us personally, much less what happens in the outside world of news events. That is what dictators try to do and they all eventually fail.

And here I am not referring to our own complex inner filters or the neuroses that we ourselves project outside ourselves on the movie screen of life and then intently watch. Rather I am talking about outside events that are actually independent of us and our mental projections, events that we can't help but react to; we do this all the time.

You and I can't control outside events (what happens to us), but we do have a choice in how we respond to these external events. Our ability to respond is what, of course, is called 'responsibility', a quality much valued in this society. Although everyone has some kind of response to life, not everyone is considered 'responsible'. We can try to learn the correct response to an infinite series of possible events by rote or we can learn to be more generally responsible. This is what employers so desperately look for when they are hiring, someone who is responsible, who naturally has the ability to respond to events in a useful fashion. Trust me, they get the promotions!

And I am making the distinction here between responding and reacting. A simple reaction is not enough; we all do that. We cannot help but react to outside events, but it is 'how' we react that determines whether we react in a so-called 'responsible' manner.

Again: we can't control what happens to us in the outside world; we can only control our own reaction, the way 'we' respond to it. In low-level jobs there frequently is an attempt to anticipate every possible event and train the employee how to respond, as I mentioned, by rote. Of course, since there are infinite possibilities, that approach can only go so far.

Much better is to find someone with an ability to respond to all situations, someone who is naturally responsible. This is, of course, an employer's dream. So what am I driving at here?

My point is that it is possible to develop our sense of responsibility to the point where we can naturally just respond to events in a useful (responsible) way.

For example, when someone is angry at us and says or does something hurtful or rude, instead of setting off a domino-effect chain-reaction of anger in response, we can learn to consider the source (they are upset or angry) and just respond appropriately. We can't control them, but we can learn to control our reaction and response to them. This is the essence of many dharma teachings, what is called 'skillful means," responding skillfully.

In almost every case, instead of reacting to the rain of problems that life too often presents to us in a defensive manner (protecting ourselves from them), if we could instead receive and just handle them responsibly, it would be so much better.... for us and the outside world.

It is all a matter of awareness, of learning to catch ourselves before we over-react and start to push back, and instead facilitate and respond to incoming events in a useful manner, like not letting life push our buttons. Awareness training is the single most valuable tool I have yet found.

Our awareness is what makes us able to respond; we are aware of the situation. Some people are born more aware and they are naturally responsible. The rest of us can develop our awareness until we become more responsible. Either way, IMO the key to how we make our way through life (career) is our ability to respond.

Reactive Alchemy

Like going to school for a single class or to church only on Sunday for an hour, with that amount of practice we get what we pay for. An hour or so a week gets us an hour or so a week of training, nothing more. Think it through. If we practiced an hour a week on guitar, we would not exactly be the musician we envisioned.

I don't intend this to sound too harsh, but even an hour a day of practice leaves 23 hours to unravel what we have done and generally accumulate karma. Part-time solutions seldom satisfy full-time needs.

I knew early on I needed to spend more time than that on mind training, but who has the time? In truth, it was not only the time, but also the tedium and boredom I often experienced just sitting there struggling with my mind, usually waiting for the clock to run out. It was pretty much self-defeating and I had no idea then that the struggle was a good sign! Dharma practice should not really be clocked. So what's the solution?

Obviously the solution requires more (not less) time spent, but perhaps in short bursts. Most of the great meditation teachers and texts say to do many short sessions rather than one long session. And they say that we should be careful not to overstay a session by pushing it longer than we feel like. Sure, we can push the limits to see if we like it, but if we don't like it, if we want to cut and run, that is not a good sign. In that case we need to regroup. A certain amount of joy, at least enthusiasm, is required to practice dharma properly. So what are our options?

I already mentioned many short sitting-meditation sessions, but that may be difficult to arrange, fraught with scheduling problems and perhaps self-consciousness. What is needed is a method to practice whenever and wherever we are that does not draw undue attention to itself. Fortunately there is a handy and portable solution at hand, your own moment-to-moment reactions.

It was no accident that my Tibetan dharma teacher (with whom I have been working with for 30+ years now) did not first suggest that I learn basic sitting meditation (Shamata). Instead he pointed out a technique called Tong-len in a Tibetan text and suggested I might practice that.

Now Tong-len, when done properly, is a complete dharma practice that we can do anywhere and anytime, so it is very portable. And it is a perfect example of Buddhist psychology, which can involve going against what we would think is the usual flow, going counter to what our personal preference might be. Our self is used to always going for the good stuff, getting more of whatever we like, not less, and certainly not giving anything away. It is almost like the prime rule of self is that we can always add more attachments, but never take any of them away. Left to its own devices, self-attachment is cumulative.

But Tong-len looks the ego right in the eye and suggests just the opposite, to give out with the good stuff and take in what we normally would totally avoid, like the suffering and pain of others that we see in this world. With Tong- len practice we send the best that we have in us out to another, and take in all of the pain and suffering that they have on ourselves. This is not something most of us would think to do, right? It is counter-intuitive to our upbringing.

However, in Buddhist psychology Tong-len is an express route to spiritual growth, a complete form of meditation all by itself. And it is a lot easier for westerners to learn than basic sitting meditation. I am not going to say much here about how the whole idea of Tong-len freaked me out when I first read about it. I have told the story several times in blogs, but it sure disturbed me. It was counter to everything I had been taught up to that point. And I am not even going to go into much detail about the practice of classical Tong-len. I wrote about it and there are many articles which you can find on the web in many places. Pema Chödrön is an expert on Tong- len, and what she writes is accurate.

Suffice it to say that IMO Tong-len is tailor-made for Americans and, better yet, we all already kind of instinctively know how to do it. What I want to explain here is a subset of standard Tong-len. But those of you who respond to this idea, by all means learn the classic Tong-len as traditionally taught, because it is very powerful and totally useful. What I present here is but a refinement, but it may be an easier approach for many of us.

I learned this method from my first true dharma teacher, who shared with me a little trick he did with a piece of string. The secret was that you could add on as much string as you wanted, but you could never take any string away that was once given. At the time I wondered why he would bother with such a trick, but over time I found the profundity in it. And here is the key.

In western psychology the emphasis is often on removing self-attachments by force, often before we are willing to give them up. Deny ourselves, diet, etc. Tong-len (on the other hand) takes the opposite approach. Self-attachment is removed not by limiting our attachments, but rather by expanding what we identify as self until we identify the entire world (and everyone in it) as part of our self. The more our self becomes identified with everything and everyone, the less hold our attachments have on us and they begin to break down and we see through them. The self eventually implodes. There is no more "self and others," because others have become part of our self. What a brilliant solution to an age-old problem! It is worth thinking this through.

In essence, Tong-len is a method to identify that which we don't already identify with, like everything "else" in the world outside ourselves, especially what we positively reject or don't like -- the "them" is not "me" kind of thing. In other words, as I present it here, this form of Tong-len is about pinpointing our reactions and doing something about transforming them incrementally and on the spot. And it is true alchemy that gives a pure result.

Like all mind training techniques, Tong-len depends on awareness to make it work, so it does require that we wake up enough to notice our own reactions, like if we flinch when someone we really don't like walks into the room. That's a reaction. But it does not have to be another person. It can be a thing or an event, like the wince that comes when we remember we have a dentist appointment -- that kind of experience.

If we wake up to our reactions and begin to watch them carefully, we have a chance to identify and make friends with parts of ourselves that we have somehow excluded from what we could call the inner circle of our self. And I am not talking about an isolated event or two a day. If we are aware, we find ourselves reacting almost constantly to all kinds of stuff all day long. These reactions are perfect opportunities for dharma practice and we can't seem to avoid them anyway. They offer a very rich field of opportunity for transformation.

The point I like to keep in mind is that each reaction that we have is recording its karma in our mindstream. Of course karma leaves its mark, but that is not the whole of it. Karma is also a seed that always grows and ripens in the future. Therefore, every time we react negatively to someone or something, we not only lay down a track in our mindstream, but we reinforce (or underline) that mark by repetition and guarantee that this very thing we try to push away from us will reappear in a larger and stronger version down the line. That is just how it works. And karma grows exponentially, not linearly.

So "reactive Tong-len" is the practice of becoming aware of what we react to, making friends with it, and eventually no longer recording that particular reaction as karma that will (literally) haunt us down the line. If you want to remove the accumulation of loads of karma, monitoring your reactions as described here is a good way to go. And it is so portable. We can do it on or off the cushion, anywhere we are, and all the time. It adds up to real practice beyond what we might otherwise be able to do. And the best thing is that no time is wasted. This may perhaps be the perfect post- meditation dharma practice.

Now I am sure to get a comment or two that this method is all about us, and very selfish on our part, just freeing ourselves from recording more karma. What about helping other people? The answer is very simple. Certainly any person that you make friends with in your mind, that you used to dislike, benefits from your practice. And until we deconstruct the self and its attachments, until they are transparent, we will never gain greater clarity.

And my Buddhist teachers have always encouraged me to first become less attached myself and then try to help others, and not vice versa. Instead, the accent is always on our own practice until such time as we free ourselves and become clear enough to actually be of use to others, and not to just muck things up more than they already are.

Anyway, I have found that monitoring my reactions, recognizing what I am habitually excluding or find negative, and then soothing or making friends with that part of myself is enormously beneficial. And it is portable and easy to do. And best of all, once we identify with our negativities and neutralize them, we no longer record that particular karma. Clarity improves.

Sometimes it is good to start small and work outward, like dropping a pebble in a still pond. As with the "string trick" mentioned earlier, "if you can't beat em', join em'," meaning: if we can't remove our attachments by attrition, try expanding what we include as our self by identifying our negative reactions, making friends with them, and including them as part of who we think we are. It is like blowing up the balloon of the self until it bursts of its own accord by inclusion instead of denial.

Is this not worth trying?

Sending and Receiving: Tong-len

Tong-len is a Tibetan Buddhist method everyone would do well to learn whether they practice dharma or not. It is that useful! And it is easy to understand and practice. Equally important, tong-len is a practice we can do anytime and anywhere. It is portable.

Tong-len is also known by the name "Sending and Receiving" as well as "Exchanging Yourself for Others, or simply "Giving and Taking." It is similar to the Christian motto "Do unto others as you would have them do unto you," and with tong-len we make the first move. We give. And the Buddhists take it to another whole level. Tong-len helps to develop compassion in an organic and very natural way. And the technique is very simple:

When we encounter another person who is suffering or in pain, we simply breathe in (mentally that is) all of their suffering and pain; we take it on or into ourself and we breathe out all our goodness, kindness, happiness, and good will back into them. In other words, we send all our goodness to them and receive from them all of their pain and suffering. We take this (again: mentally) on ourself. This is considered perhaps the quickest method to seriously increase a sense of compassion and to decrease ingrained selfishness. And this can also be done with any world situation, a plane crash, an earthquake, and so on, anywhere there is suffering. Seeing others in pain and suffering is not the only use for this valuable technique. It also works to clear our own personal obscurations on an item by item basis.

In other words, it works equally well for when we encounter people who are angry at us, irritating us, pissing us off, or whatever. The technique is the same. You simply breathe in (mentally) all that which is 'other' or different and separate from you in the other person and breathe out and back to them all of the goodness and joy in yourself, whatever you can muster at the time. In other words, we breathe into our self all of the dark, bad, painful, offensive, and "otherness" and we breathe out all that is good, kind, and happy in ourself. From the Western viewpoint this is counter-intuitive, exactly the opposite of what most of us have been taught, which is to keep the good things close and keep the "bad" things as far away as possible.

In tong-len we send to others (exchange with them) all our well-being, happiness, goodness, and receive from them all of their darkness, sadness, pain, suffering, nastiness, and whatever it is that 'we' have labeled or can label as "other" in them. And we do this again and again and again until some equilibrium is achieved between the two of us in our mind. They (the other person) won't even be aware of this, so don't look for them to change their expression. You are detoxing 'your' fear and reaction to them, not their own to you. Sounds scary, no?

When I first read about this technique I thought for all the world that tong-len was a medieval throwback from the Dark Ages. As an astrologer who counseled others for many years I had been taught by western psychics to do just the opposite to tong-len, to get as far away from other's pain as possible and to not take it on personally. I had been told to always wash my hands in running water after a personal reading and imagine all the pain, nastiness, and what-not that I might have picked up from my client going down the drain with the water. Tong-len is 180-degrees different from that approach and this was at first very hard for me to appreciate and accept. Frankly I wanted to cut and run.

I am glad I did not because this highly-efficient technique is spot-on as an antidote for our western tendency to isolate ourselves from others and brand them as 'bad' or at least separate from ourselves. And tong-len is perhaps the quickest and most direct way to extend our own boundaries to include something else beyond our own skin as in: family, friends.... all those other than ourselves.

Tong-len is also useful beyond just those we encounter who are suffering and in pain or who irritate or make us angry. That is just the tip of the iceberg for this technique. People we react to strongly in a negative way aside, tong-len is brilliant as a tool to neutralize whatever confronts us from the outside, whatever we have labeled as different or "other" from ourselves -- everything we have marked as "bad" since our childhood, every attitude we have perhaps unconsciously adopted that separates us from the world around us and send us into a karma- making tailspin every time it appears to us.

All of these are expertly handled with a little tong-len practice. And while proper sitting meditation technique is something that can require time and commitment, most Americans take to tong-len right off. They just "get" the concept straight away and start using it. It is that simple.

In summary, tong-len is an easy technique that can be learned almost at once and that can be used not only on the mediation cushion but anytime and anywhere during the rest of our day. What tong-len effectively does is extend the perimeter of what we consider to be our ourselves outward to include more and more of the outside world, a world that 'we' have labeled as "other" than ourselves or for whatever reason just "bad."

With just a little training in tong-len we learn to become aware every time we catch ourselves labeling another person as someone to close-off and shut out, and we reverse the process. We accept and take them in, essentially making friends with ourselves, because somewhere along the line we have closed the door on that person, food, attitude, or what-have- you? Tong-len opens that door again.

And doing tong-len with people is only part of what this technique can handle. Any attitude, prejudice, hatred, fear, competitiveness, jealousy, etc. that we become aware of in ourselves can be neutralized with this technique. Notice that key phrase "that we become aware of," because for tong-len to work we have to focus not on the thing we "hate" or react to and then follow that feeling, but rather we focus on the awareness that here is something that "we" hate or don't like. Got it?

For example, if I hate being called "Mike" instead of "Michael," and you just called me 'Mike," I focus my awareness of my reaction to what you just said rather than what you just said and make sure not to follow the reaction and launch into setting you straight with more emotion than it is worth. In other words, we learn to recognize when something is "other" or pops into our view reactively. We catch our reaction. Rather than react, we drop it, and do tong-len with our own reaction. This type of tong-len also helps to remove our prejudices and obscurations one at a time.

With tong-len we gradually extend the limits of our dislikes and prejudices outward much like when a drop of water strikes the surface of a calm lake, concentric circles open and reach out in ever-expanding rings beyond the drop. We become ever more inclusive.

Neutralizing the separation and otherness between ourselves and the world around us brings enormous benefits. By ending the isolation and separateness (the so-called labeling and prejudice), we get back all of the energy we have locked in holding on to these prejudices and biases all this time. Better yet, once we have neutralized this labeling, we instantly stop creating all of this difficult karma in our mindstream and that stream begins to clear. Remember that every time we invoke a negative reaction to something, even if it is a legitimate gripe, we dig a deeper karmic track in our own mindstream, one that will take more and more work to eventually neutralize or erase.

It does not matter if we have a 'right' to get mad at whatever or whomever offends or confronts us. What matters is that when we do get mad, we only add insult to the injury we may have received by the imagined (or real) affront, internalizing I, and recording it ever deeper in our mindstream. Every hatred, prejudice, bias, fear, and doubt that we have locked up in the world that we imagine as outside us is a reflection of an attitude we maintain inside us. We are the one hurt by it. Each instance takes another little piece of our life energy.

When each bias and attitude is gradually removed, our mind is clearer and our energy greater. And, as mentioned, we are no longer digging our own karmic grave by endlessly reinforcing the trace or track of that "otherness" in our mindstream. It really is a win/win situation, and it is so easy.

Tong-len is the great equalizer and neutralizer. It is perhaps the first Buddhist mind-practice technique those new to the dharma should consider. When I was introduced to tong-len, it scared the bejesus out of me at first glance. But after trying it even for a short while I recognized it for the powerful antidote from my negative attachments that it is.

Tong-len: How I came to Learn It

In a previous article I described Tong-len, the powerful Tibetan Buddhist mind practice for developing compassion and paring the ego down to size, not to mention that it helps to remove the myriad of biases and prejudices we inherit from our society or manage to develop ourselves. Here is the story of how I first encountered tong-len many years ago.

I had met this wonderful Tibetan lama (a rinpoche) during a visit of his to Ann Arbor, Michigan and Margaret (my wife) and I were so moved by that meeting that we had to see him again, Khenpo Karthar Rinpoche lived high in the mountains above Woodstock, New York and it was the dead of winter. In fact it was during those weird bardo-like days after Christmas and before the New Year. We all know those days. My wife and I piled our three kids (at the time) into our little car and began an 800-mile drive across the country in a frigid cold spell. Our youngest daughter was only about one and one half years old at the time and normally we would not take such a young child that far away from home in the bitter cold. But we did. That was how important it was for us to meet this rinpoche again. We knew we could learn from this man and we were hungry for a change in our lives.

It was a long trip that took two days and by early evening of the second day we had reached Woodstock, New York. Darkness had set in and the cold was so intense that then entire front inside windshield of the car was frosted over; I was using a business card to scrape a tiny hole in the frosted glass to peer out of. We were driving up the narrow three-mile mountain road to the Buddhist center. It was slow going and we were not sure what we would find when we finally got there. Finally, we pulled into a small parking lot outside of a large building that used to be a resort hotel. It had seen better days. This was before the monastery was built, although they were beginning to pour the foundation when winter had set in.

We got out of the car and the little group of us stood huddled by the door and knocking. A high wind on the mountain was blowing sharp as we waited. It was dark and there were no outside lights. At last someone came and the door was opened by a very nice lady; we were invited inside. I guess I should tell you now that we had no appointment. No one knew we were coming. We just had winged it. Even so, the lady (her name was Norvie) was very kind and led us into a small waiting room; she would tell the rinpoche and see if he was available.

I will spare you the whole story of that visit and just cut to the chase to save space here. Suffice it to say that the Rinpoche was very kind, but firm. I wanted to know what I should do in order to become his student. Margaret felt similarly. We liked him that much! And pushy me, because I had been an astrologer and done "spiritual" things for many years, I was hoping to place out of "meditation 101" and get right to the advanced stuff. That tells you how foolish I was. Rinpoche very gently told me that he could see that I had never harmed anyone with my astrology, but that when it came to learning meditation, because I knew little to nothing about it (and had done little to nothing with it so far) that it was best if I started at the very beginning. This, he said, would be the fastest way.

The fastest way? Well, I had to think twice about that because my arrogance was acting up again, but I respected this man so much that I was willing to do just as he said. OK, I would start at the beginning. And now I am getting to the point about Tong-len here.

When we were about to leave, Rinpoche gave us a small book called "The Torch of Certainty" by a high lama named Jamgon Kongtrul Lodro Thaye Rinpoche (1830-1899). Later I discovered this was one of the classic mind- training texts used in the Karma Kagyu Lineage. And Rinpoche pointed out the section on Tong-len for us to consider, the technique I described earlier.

When Rinpoche had said goodbye and was gone we went back outside. In the dark, we could see the bare cement walls of the monastery being built and the high winds were whipping the plastic covering that was hanging from the newly poured cement. It was a little eerie and there were no stars out. Anyway, we drove our little car slowly back down the mountain and managed to find a motel in Woodstock where we could stay the night.

There we were, crammed into one room that had a single (and very small) infrared wall heater that barely kept the bitter cold outside where it belonged. Anyway, there with our little kids we opened this small book and began to read the section on tong-len, a technique we certainly had never heard of before. And it was a shocker.

Maybe it was just the night and the fact that we were huddled together around a tiny heater (with our babies) 800 miles from home on one of the most bitter winter nights of that year. What this book said was to breathe into yourself all the darkness and suffering in the world and breathe back out whatever good feeling and well-being you had. In fact the tong-len technique is often simply translated as "Exchanging Yourself for Others."

Well this suggestion went 180-degrees against what every spiritual person and technique had taught me up to that point. In fact, I had been taught to not take in anything dark, negative, or fear-filled, and to keep such things as far away from me as possible. Psychics had even shown me how to wash my hands after doing an astrology reading for a client and let the harmful and negative thoughts that might otherwise accumulate just go down the drain. So tong-len was saying just the opposite and I mean totally the opposite: that I was to breathe in the bad stuff and give others or whatever was out there any good stuff I had. What?

I know Margaret and I looked each other in the eye and wondered what had we gotten ourselves into? It was scary and very hard to get our mind around it. At first my gut feeling was to just cut and run and to get the hell out of there. Yet here we were, shivering together in this tiny hotel room so far from home. There was no instant solution. But we read on. We had nothing else to do.

Gradually we learned that tong-len, despite how it appeared to us at the time, was an advanced shortcut to compassion and the handling of suffering and negativity. All my life I had tried to keep as far away from anything negative (people and things) as I could. I mean: who wants that? And here was a technique telling me to do just the opposite, to welcome and breathe all this bad stuff into me and exchange it in the out-breath for whatever good stuff, feelings, and thoughts I had. These Tibetans get right to the heart every time. It got my attention.

Well, we got through the night, back on the road, and finally made it all way the home and with the concept of tong-len still intact. We would give it a try and we did. So there you have the story of how we came upon tong-len.

Tong-len has turned out to be an incredible and efficient method to remove obscurations and all the mental prejudice that we have accumulated, including those that society has gifted us with by just being born in the particular where and when we were. And unlike sitting meditation, which I found quite difficult to obtain results from, tong-len was easy to learn and do. All it required was that I gradually become more aware of my own negative reactions, biases, and preconceptions. Instead of simply following them as I had all my life, I learned to recognize and neutralize them as they arose using the tong-len technique. I made friends with my own enemies and gradually removed the walls of my personality.

Here I have given you kind of a short-hand introduction to tong-len. It would be best to learn it formally from a teacher, if you can. There are also other considerations that are very important, like making aspirations (intent) before you begin and dedicating the merit of whatever practice you do to benefit all sentient beings, that kind of thing. I have covered those elsewhere in a book called "Dharma: The Intangibles," which can be found as a free e- book here.

http://spiritgrooves.net/e-Books.aspx

Tong-len: Mental Feng-Shui

Let's say I see a small puppy or child being hurt or suffering. It is quite natural for my heart go out to such an innocent creature. I am instantly compassionate. I wish I could lessen the suffering and take that small creature in my arms and hold it, giving it comfort. Tong-len is like this.

We recognize and take on the suffering or pain wherever we find it and send back all that we have that might be comforting and kind. As mentioned, our heart goes out in these situations. This is the process. And while it is easier to imagine with something like a hurt puppy, the same transaction can be practiced with all who suffer, and should be. This is what tong-len is all about, regardless of whether the object is a cute puppy or a gnarly old what-have-you. All beings are deserving of compassion, even more so if they are mean and hurtful. Somewhere in there someone is suffering.

And while learning to have compassion wherever suffering is found is where tong-len shines, it can have other practical uses throughout our life each day. It is easy to see where we would have compassion for a hurt child or puppy, but perhaps less easy to see where we ourselves are constantly hurt, often by our own biases and prejudices.

It can be as obvious as the not-so-friendly co-worker that we suddenly meet as we round an office corner. What is our reaction? You know what it is. There is nothing kind about it and we tend to react with dislike and probably fear of the unknown. It can be painful when we know someone has singled us out and made a point of not liking us. When they suddenly appear in our day, the tendency is to shrink back and put up defenses. Am I right? Use your own words.

Tong-len would have us do just the reverse from reacting in fear or dislike. Instead we open up and take in all that we fear or loathe, breathe it in, and absorb it, and then send back whatever we can manage that is kind and open in return. It would seem that we are being vulnerable by doing so, but in fact it is we who become stronger through the process. This is what tong-len is all about. This is mind training folks!

Our prejudices and biases define the boundary between what we consider safe (our Self) and everything 'other' outside ourselves. When we do tong-len in a situation, we are gradually moving those boundaries between self and other so that we are more inclusive and embracing of others. What was once 'other' is slowly weakened and eventually vanishes, becoming known and a part of us. We have made friends with the 'other' parts of ourselves. We are more inclusive.

Tong-len is exactly the opposite of being divisive or polarizing. It weakens and breaks down duality rather than strengthening it. Instead of reinforcing fear and hatred, tong-len gradually removes the otherness out there somewhere and reclassifies it as part of ourselves, as something now known. We are making friends with ourselves through tong-len.

Are the others we are doing tong-len for (and with) helped by our action? They are certainly not hurt by it, and the fact that it makes us a friendlier and more compassionate being can't help but be useful to all who have to come to know us. I would say, yes, it is helpful to others as well as us. Let me summarize please.

Many of us are busy; we don't manage to find enough time for sitting meditation and/or we may not have done enough meditation to begin to reap the rewards of doing so. Sitting meditation takes practice time until a habit is formed that can really be of use to us. Tong-len is something we can do at anytime and anywhere. It does not take long and we don't have to interrupt whatever else we are doing. And it works.

Tong-len need not only be a somewhat drawn-out affair with lots of breathing in and breathing out. We only do tong-len until we feel that we have weakened, neutralized, and otherwise softened the duality we experience, the 'us' and 'them' of it, until we make friends with that other part of ourselves.

It can also be used for smaller and smaller events like winces, grimaces, and so one, whatever we come across in a moment that provokes us. In fact, tong-len is like mental Feng Shui in that when we encounter something that disturbs or upsets us we change its location from outside our mandala to within our mandala. Tong-len allows us to rearrange our self just as Feng Shui lets us rearrange our home.

What about Hate and Fear?

This is about dealing with what we hate and fear in life – a superior way to work with these. It is clear from comments from students that most of you know something about meditation. It is equally clear from your notes here that not many of you have even heard about "Tong-len," which is a totally different (and equally valuable) Tibetan mind- training technique from that of sitting meditation.

Tong-len has to do with our personal mandala, the mini-world we have created around ourselves, what we include in that world, and what we consider as definitely outside of that world. And while Tong-len can be done while sitting on a cushion (like meditation), it is most often done off-the-cushion while we are walking around doing our everyday things.

We can use it all the time.

Tong-len has to do with the people and things we don't like, whatever comes up on our radar screen that is "other," awful, threatening, or just different. It is also an approach to all the suffering in the world, but I will get to that. This technique is particularly useful when we "hate" something or are repulsed by a person, event, or thing. Sound useful? It is very useful. In fact I am surprised that more folks don't know about it.

Along with regular sitting meditation, tong-len is part of the mental toolbox of every Tibetan Buddhist. For some reason here in the West most people have never heard of it, much less learned how to use it. Let's rectify that now. I have to warn you that Tong- len (from a western perspective) is a radical technique. In this sense it is advanced. It is so direct that it scared the bejesus out of me when I first heard about it. I wanted to run screaming from the thought and I almost did, so be prepared for something a little different.

The idea of Tong-len is very simple and it has to do with your personal mandala, what you consider yourself and what you consider not yourself – outside you. It has to do with when you encounter anything outside yourself, anything other, foreign, negative, opposite, "bad", scary, horrible, hideous, etc. When you recognize something as definitely "not- you," instead of crossing your fingers at it and trying to keep it at a distance, you do just the opposite.

Instead of pushing it away, you pull it toward you; you breathe and take it in. You absorb it willingly and in return send out, breathe out, and let go of all that is good, kind, loving, fresh, fine, etc., inside you. You send that back in exchange for all that bad stuff. This is true for anything you consider outside yourself, especially if it inspires fear, loathing, disgust, hatred, anger, or what-have-you – any "otherness." The concept is easy to grasp.

And you don't just breathe in and out just once, but continually until you have neutralized or normalized or made friends with whatever is outside. Of course you do this with whatever suffering you see in the world. You take on the pain and suffering, breathe it in, and breathe out or send your goodwill and kindness back out. And you do this anytime you find yourself being critical, judgmental, nasty, mean, and so on to something outside yourself, something "not you." I could go on, but let me summarize.

Tong-len is an incredible technique for removing duality, otherness, and extending our personal mandala or world view to accept and in fact embrace more and more of what has been shut out by us as "otherness."

Just think about it and (more important) try it. This is a shortcut to greater compassion and kindness.

As to whether breathing in all this darkness, anger, and negativity is physically harmful? It is not. In fact, it removes your own negativity by shifting the limits of your tolerance in the direction of greater compassion and acceptance.

Tong-len is taught and used hand-in-hand in Tibetan Buddhist mind training along with sitting meditation. These are the two main pillars of practice. Tong-len is a brilliant way to gradually remove whatever separates you from the real world around you. You can do it all day long wherever you are and whenever you encounter anything strange or "other." You can do Tong-len and start right on the spot to make friends with whatever is out there and perceived as other, alien, or against you.

It is especially good with enemies or not-so-friends. Instead of shutting them out and taking offence, you open up to them, take in whatever offends you, and give out kindness, goodwill, and your own good energy. You do all of this in your mind, but physical hugging and kindness is also allowed. Check this most potent technique out for yourself. Try tong-len.

Overload

[This is a related article, emotional overloads, a perfect candidate for tong-len practice.]

Now here is a touchy issue, my own emotional upheavals. When I discover (I don't always even know) that I am emotionally upset by something, I have learned I must be much more careful than usual. Years ago I had a little mantra that I whispered to myself: "We will withstand shocks out- breaking." I have no idea who I meant by "we," but I guess it was all of us. Anyway, back then (much like now) emotional shocks of one sort of another were always breaking out. Let's face it; some things in life (even little things) are hard to take, especially if we are sensitive.

I never know when an emotional load might suddenly land on my shoulders and overload my capacitors. My first dharma teacher used to say "I have no pot to piss in," meaning he had nowhere to unload the charge that I am sure he must have carried at times. He did not want to just dump on those around him.

Unfortunately that is what most of us do. We can't help ourselves. The overload just spills over and usually on to those nearest to us, often the ones we love and cherish the most. And it can happen like lightning.

I receive some bad news or something upsets me. Of course I try to manage it, but as often as not it is going to take me some time to process this bit of upset and there I am, right in the middle of whatever I am doing, perhaps surrounded by my family or other people. The last thing I want to do is unload this charge onto someone else, but I am too proud to stop the presses and tell everyone I am having a problem.

Often I don't have time (or don't want to make it public) that I am carrying a charge from somewhere, something, and perhaps someone else that has nothing to do with where I am right now or whomever I am with. Despite attempts on my part to control, my upset just escapes me and before I know it I have dumped the charge (the whole load) onto what otherwise would be a normal communication, charging the whole moment. It can get heavy like that real fast.

Of course, I should immediately apologize and acknowledge that I am under some kind of stress, but too often I try to contain myself and not burden others with what are obviously my problems. And there is the pride issue too. Keeping quiet about it would be fine if I COULD contain myself and if some lightning rod of a moment didn't discharge me onto a friend or family member. Bam! The harm is already done.

Before I know it I have created a situation that demands an apology on my part, and if those around me react with shock or hurt at what I have just laid on them (and they react in turn), the whole scene escalates into a full-scale drama and sometimes all hell breaks loose.

Often, before I know it, I too am taking offence and the original discharge is lost in the general carpet bombing going on around me. It is worse if I don't acknowledge where it is coming from, i.e. me.

I wish I could just issue a warning if I am carrying a loaded charge, like "Get back folks, I'm losing it," but that seldom happens and the overload just slips out and charges the atmosphere. If I could be out front about what is happening, perhaps then others could give me a little latitude as I try to manage my own emotions. However, if I try to keep it private and then lose control, this is really unfair to those around me.

When my feelings get hurt or something untoward happens, it is very difficult not to end up with a charge that won't quickly dissipate. And it can be one of those all-day suckers that will take time for me to work through until it trickles down to anything normal. The bigger the front, the bigger the back.

In the meantime, the best I can do is try to steer clear of other people, but that is not always easy either, especially with family whom otherwise I have encouraged to be near. Even if I announce that I am under a heavy charge, this is not always enough. I try to get off by myself and let it all blow over because close proximity can be explosive when I am upset, but somehow the charge is still communicated and fills the air. All of a sudden, everyone is walking on pins and needles.

And I am not the only one with this problem. As a counselor for more years than I want to mention, this phenomenon is epidemic and worldwide. The Buddhists call these emotional upheavals, kleshas, and they also point out that they are very difficult to remove.

And these emotional events happen so organically. There I am, happy as a clam, and I get some bad news or take offense at something that someone does or says. All of a sudden I am overwhelmed with emotion, just fully charged, not expecting it, and unable to control it well enough. I try.

And the sad thing is that the first person that appears in my wake becomes the lightning rod and gets the discharge, often the full load. It could be our dog who did something wrong or perhaps my wife or kids who just happened to wander into the room. Before I know it I get heavy-handed and what otherwise would be a simple remark on my part becomes a loaded remark, one that sets off a war of words or whatever.

To make matters worse, I too often try to contain it rather than acknowledge it, but the cat is already out of the bag, the harm done. If I would instantly apologize and admit my upset, it would help. But at those times it seems I can't bring myself to cop to it and instead continue to think I can manage what is already obviously unmanageable.

As mentioned, if I would humble myself enough to communicate to those around me that I am upset, they would comfort me I am sure. I could have an orderly discharge and de-escalation. I would feel better too. Pride on my part does not help. Bottling all this stuff up results in anger and attempts to contain it lead to explosions -- a vicious cycle.

These kind of upsets for many of us are not about to stop happening, I am sure. They can be remedied, but the remedy takes a lot of work on my part to apprehend my hair-trigger reactions and learn to respond to bad news or insult differently, to not take it so personally. That will take time, and I am working on it. Buddhist mind training and the awareness it brings has been the most helpful. Meanwhile, I am doing my best to fess up to those around me when I get a sudden overload.

Does this ring a bell and how do you folks handle this?

For more free materials (e-books, articles, and videos) see:

http://dharmagrooves.com

YouTube

http://www.youtube.com/user/merlewine?feature=watch

iTunes: Podcasts under "Spirit Grooves"

SkyBrite:

https://www.skybrite.com/php/

Michael@Erlewine.net

Printed in Great Britain
by Amazon